Y0-DWN-749

Dollars and Cents

by Jamie A. Schroeder

Table of Contents

I need to know these words.

coins

dimes

dollar

nickels

pennies

quarters

3

How Many Pennies Do You Need?

The boy sees a kite. The kite costs one dollar. The girl sees a jump rope. The jump rope costs one dollar.

 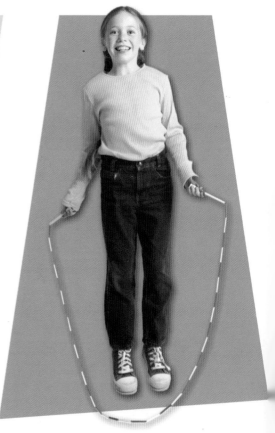

▲ Each child has some money.

The children have pennies.
The children can use the pennies
to buy things.

▲ This child has many pennies.

This girl wants a balloon. A balloon costs one dollar. One penny is equal to one cent. One dollar is equal to one hundred pennies.

▲ This girl has 100 pennies.

How can you write about money?
You can use symbols.

WORDS	SYMBOL
cent	¢
is equal to	=
dollar	$

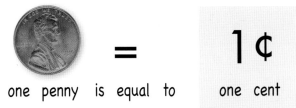

one penny   is equal to   one cent

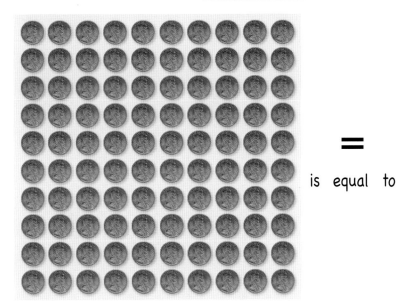

$1.00

one dollar

is equal to

▲ One hundred pennies is equal to one dollar.

7

What Other Coins Do You Need?

The boy wants to buy a baseball. The baseball costs one dollar. The boy has twenty nickels.

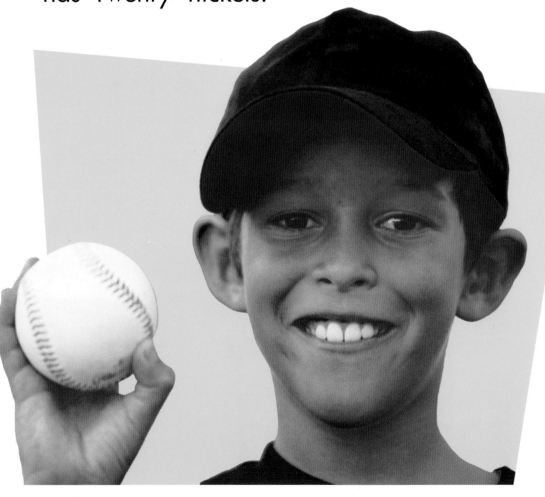

▲ Does the boy have $1.00?

One nickel is equal to five cents.
Twenty nickels is equal to one dollar.

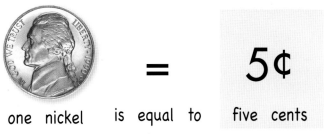

one nickel   is equal to   five cents

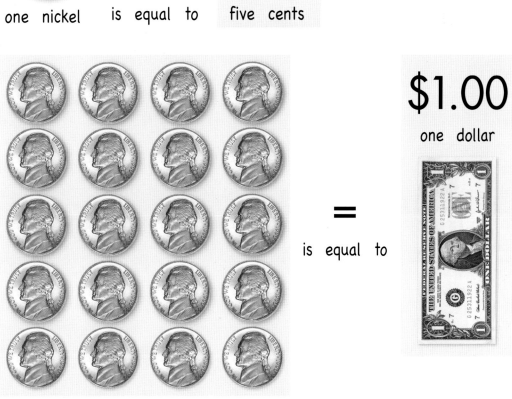

▲ Twenty nickels is equal to $1.00.

The girl has ten dimes. The girl wants to buy a drink. The drink costs one dollar. Does she have enough money?

▲ The girl has enough money to buy a drink.

One dime is equal to ten cents.
Ten dimes is equal to one dollar.

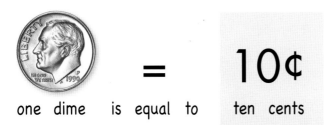

one dime   is equal to   ten cents

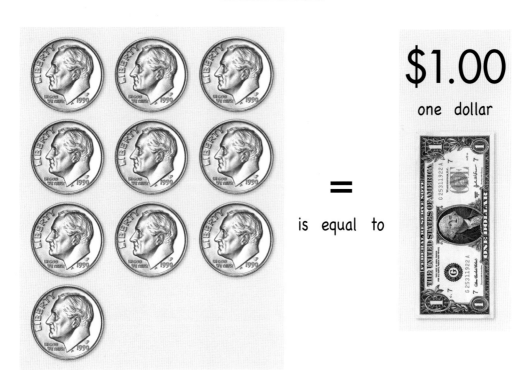

$1.00

one dollar

is equal to

▲ Ten dimes is equal to $1.00.

The boy wants to buy a cookie.
The cookie costs one dollar. He has
four coins. The coins are quarters.

▲ Can the boy buy a cookie?

One quarter is equal to twenty-five cents.
Four quarters is equal to one dollar.

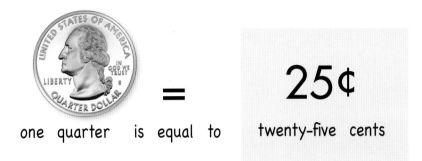

one quarter   is equal to   twenty-five cents

$1.00

one dollar

is equal to

▲ Four quarters is equal to one dollar.

How Can You Use Different Coins?

The girl wants to buy ice cream. The ice cream costs one dollar. The girl has different coins.

▲ Can the girl buy ice cream?

The girl adds the quarters first.
Then the girl adds the dimes.
She adds the pennies last.

75¢ + 20¢ + 5¢

$1.00

one dollar

=

is equal to

You have two quarters and two dimes.
You also have four nickels and
ten pennies. How much money do
you have?